GOING FROM HOBBY TO BUSINESS ON ETSY

Book 3 of *The Ultimate Guide to Selling On Etsy* Series

by Noelle Ihli and Jeanne Allen

CONTENTS

CONTENTS

A QUICK NOTE

At the very end of this book, you'll find a link that will direct you to an offer page for the University of Etsy (our video courses!) exclusively for our readers.

The University of Etsy (by yours truly, CraftRanker!) is made up of more than 90 in-depth instructional videos and worksheets that enhance and reinforce book learning and help you apply what you've learned about starting a successful Etsy shop.

These standalone video courses would be $247 at full price (Think of them like a Masterclass for Etsy sellers). We're offering them as a learning companion to our readers for just 19.99.

We created these classes as a way to help friends and family who asked for help with their shops but had trouble digesting some of the concepts in book format ((It's kind of like we're sitting right next to you by the computer, taking you step by step through each concept).

While you can absolutely get everything you need to know to start a successful Etsy shop from this book (or from the University of Etsy video coursework; either is meant to be a complete resource!) many of our readers find that the video instruction is a helpful companion. If that's you, we invite you to take advantage of this offer for our readers!

INTRODUCTION

You're reading Book 3 of our series, *The Ultimate Guide to Selling on Etsy*. This three-book series will guide you through strategies for scaling growth, ramping up sales, and turning a promising Etsy shop (a part-time hobby) into a thriving business.

As a reminder (in case you need to circle back to any of the subjects we've covered in the first two volumes):

Book 2 covered everything you need to know about keywords, marketing, and advertising for Etsy specifically: Think of it as an instruction manual on how to take your solid foundation and grow your shop into something bigger. We'll teach you how to make your products more visible within Etsy and across the web, for higher sales volume and faster growth.

Book 1 was all about coaching you through the fundamentals of creating, setting up, optimizing, and operating a successful Etsy shop. If you skipped the first book (because this isn't your first rodeo with Etsy and you have a solid foundation to build on) it's no problem! This book WILL build on (and assume basic understanding) of shop setup and terminology. (Hint: That means if you need a refresher, check out Book 1! We'll wait.)

In this final book, we'll be talking a lot about growth, expansion, scaling, and business logistics. We'll share strategies for speeding up growth as you use and apply the principles in Book 1 and Book 2.

If you know you want all three books, we've also packaged them into one resource, entitled *The Ultimate Guide to Selling on Etsy*.

Now that we're oriented, let's dig in!

First of all, why did I write this book series? (If you've read the previous two books, this is going to be very familiar! But for those of you who are just jumping on board, I'll tell this story one last time!).

The Ultimate Guide to Selling on Etsy series is the culmination of everything I've learned since opening my own Etsy shop in 2013. I was a young mom with two kids, and I opened my shop as a way to carve out something that was just mine. Something that I loved to do, even if I was tired after a long day of tricking my toddlers into liking vegetables.

I had no idea what I was doing at first. But little by little, I learned. I planned. I threw spaghetti at the wall. I failed (I'll tell you all about those failures and mistakes, so you can avoid them!) I connected with other shop owners and learned what I could from them. I pored over the forums on Etsy. I experimented.

I did more of what worked. I took what I could from the failures. I kept learning. And growing

. . . Until I was so busy, that I had a decision to make. I couldn't keep my full time job and my Etsy shop because I was getting home at 5, spending time with my kids, and then working until midnight. So I made the leap. I quit my job and became a full-time Etsy shop owner. And it was one of the best decisions I ever made.

Etsy is an incredible platform. There's so much potential there. And if you know what works, you can be successful. I know because I did it.

Even if you've seen some success, you may still think of your artwork or handmade goods as your "little hobby." And I want you to knock that off right now. I've found that the people who run Etsy shops are some of the most creative, tenacious people I know. And I have no doubt that you are one of them. You can do this. You DO have what it takes.

Whether you're young or old, have 15 minutes a day to devote to your craft or hours, whether you're tech savvy or not, you can do this. I'm here to help.

That's why Jeanne and I wrote this book (Remember when I told you I found what worked? Well, Jeanne's brilliance and insight into the SEO/keyword/algorithm aspect of Etsy has worked magic in my shop. I'm going to let her introduce herself in just a bit). Jeanne and I are going to help you get started—and succeed—on Etsy as we ramp up your growth through marketing, SEO, and keyword research.

There's nothing that makes us happier than hearing feedback along the lines of "I thought this stuff would be way over my head. I'm not a marketer. But this was so easy to follow."

We promise down-to-earth, accurate, easy-to-follow information (and all confusing concepts explained!). No "secrets." No "one weird trick." Just what actually works.

Crafters are, well, crafty. They're creative and scrappy and strong. Handmade doesn't mean cute (I mean, it can). Handmade just means that you know how to roll up your sleeves and turn something ordinary into something incredible.

And that's exactly what we're here to help you do as you continue your journey on Etsy.

You've built the foundation of your Etsy house with solid shop setup, core principles, and listings that are buttoned up tight. You've learned how to advertise using keywords and SEO on Etsy and beyond. You've gotten some marketing chops! Now let's ramp up sales and put the pedal to metal on growth!

In the early days, when this moment was just a pipe dream, you probably imagined it with excitement and anticipation and maybe a little disbelief. After all, sometimes that imposter syndrome kicks in and it's difficult to believe that YOUR shop, your product could become a full-fledged business.

And when the sales start rolling in, when you find yourself busier and busier, it IS exciting. Don't get me wrong. And you should take a moment to CELEBRATE. Because behind that success is a lot of hard work. But sometimes (if you're anything like us), that excitement about growth comes with some anxieties, fear, and "what do I do about ____." Because finding yourself CEO of a snowballing business brings with it some new logistical challenges and uncharted territory.

But take a deep breath. Because everything is going to be fine. More than fine, in fact. All of your questions have answers, and all of this uncharted territory will soon be a well-mapped reality of your thriving Etsy shop.

So, let's talk about the ins and outs of setting up your business for scale, accounting, best practices for growth on Etsy, hiring (gasp!) and all the other good stuff that once sounded sort of boring but is now very, very important.

~Noelle and Jeanne

A LITTLE ABOUT US

Before we dive into the meat of this book, we want to introduce ourselves (again, you can skip this section if you've read Books 1 and 2). We hope the advice in this book feels like pointers from a good friend: tips and advice from someone who will give the good stuff to you straight. To that end, we want you to know a little about who we are as people.

Noelle

I've already told you part of my life story (the part that involves my success on Etsy), which is arguably the most important thing you need to know about me (since you're reading a book series I co-wrote called *The Ultimate Guide to Selling on Etsy*).

But again, the whole point of this book is getting the real scoop on Etsy from a real person. So in that spirit, here's a little more about me:

First of all, I'm a mom. A boy mom to Luke and Max, and a cat mom to Michelle. When I'm willing to wear pants (which is less often than I aspire to wearing them), I can be found in mom jeans.

My husband Nate is the best person I know. He's hilarious and sweet and has an adorably bald head.

The two things I love most (in addition to Etsy and the aforementioned children and husband) are murder and horses. (Separately, never together.) I'm the weird horse girl you knew in elementary school who never grew out of that phase. And I'm the person Netflix is targeting when they roll out a new serial killer documentary, which is also the reason I have a keyed lock on my bedroom door.

My degree is in Spanish translation, which I don't use but don't regret because it opens up an entire world of television to me. In addition to being a mom and Etsypreneur, I've worked "traditional" jobs in marketing, social media, writing, and editing. I don't regret them either, even though I've never looked back from my decision to pursue Etsy as my full-time job.

That's me. I'm an introvert, which means that if you ever see me on a coaching video or webinar, I am definitely sweating. But I learned a long time ago that regularly doing scary, worthwhile things is a smart way to live. So here I am.

Jeanne

Like Noelle, I'm also a mom—to Kaylee, Eileen, and Tober. (Yes, Tober. The short story is that I let Kaylee name her baby brother when she was five. I swear I would have stepped in if she'd added too many Xs or Zs, but luckily, she hadn't learned those letters yet). And my husband Bryan is, like Noelle's Nate, adorably bald and pretty dang awesome and supportive. Especially when I decided to veer off a more standard career in technical editing and jumped headfirst into the world of Etsy selling.

As for pets, our family's latest foray is to adopt two mini rex bunnies, Ginsburg and Rocky Balboa. Who knew bunnies could be such great pets or that they have such big personalities? Rocky is in the habit of picking fights with animals much bigger than himself (chickens, cats, raccoons), and I'm pretty sure Ginsburg has clinical anxiety (possibly because of Rocky. Sorry Ginzy…). I've fallen in love with them both, surprising myself, since I've never been a huge animal person.

I thrive on political podcasts, fantasy novels, and group exercise classes (I'm 100% unmotivated to move my body without someone telling me what to do). And I really, really love coffee.

My degree is in Editing and SEO, and I started out in technical editing after college. I've edited everything from textbooks to computer manuals to journal articles on aerospace engineering (a.k.a., rocket science) and earthquakes. Technical editing has its perks (it definitely pays well), but one thing it's not is very exciting (at least, not for me). Working with Noelle the last three and a half years in the Etsy shop has been so much more fun. The work we do pulls from all the technical training I've had and has given me opportunities to learn a lot of new things as well.

I love our Etsy shop, and I love Etsy as an ecommerce platform. We're here to help you feel the love (and success) on Etsy too!

CHAPTER 1

The Boring Stuff: Setting Up Your Business

Consider this chapter a sort of quick-reference for the different challenges and logistical questions you're going to run into as you grow beyond making just a few sales per month. First up, we're going to talk about business structure. This is really important, because it directly affects your bottom line profits (a.k.a., how much you have to pay in taxes). It also makes sure you're covering your bases so that you don't get audited (or if you do, you've got all your ducks in a row).

Business Designation: LLC vs. S-corp vs. Self-employed?

The biggest question most Etsy-shop owners have when they're starting out—and the decision that will affect your business and growth potential the most—is your business designation.

You might think, "But I'm super small, do I need a business designation? It's just me." And the answer is probably yes (although you don't have to be a registered business to sell on Etsy). Create an LLC as early as possible once you've started selling on Etsy, especially if this is your dream to eventually grow your shop into a sustainable business.

Start an LLC

Even if you're just doing Etsy as a part-time gig right now, you'll have access to more opportunities, better supply prices and wholesale rates if you register formally as an LLC (Limited Liability

Company) and get an EIN (Employer Identification Number). Registering as an LLC can also protect you from loss in certain situations.

We'll talk about another business designation you should (strongly) consider in a moment, but the long and short of it is this: 99% of Etsy shop owners (large and small) should form an LLC. Here's why:

- It's incredibly simple and pretty inexpensive. You'll choose a name for your LLC. If your LLC name is different from your business name, you'll also need to fill out a DBA form (Doing Business As) for your business name. E.g., my LLC name is Dynamite Gal, LLC. My DBA is Fourth Wave for my Etsy shop and CraftRanker for the coaching business that Jeanne and I run together. I did this because I wanted a more generic-sounding business name for my freelance writing and design work. Costs to officially file as an LLC vary by state, but expect to pay around $100.

- After you legally form your LLC with the Secretary of State (in your state), you'll need to apply for your EIN (Employee ID number, also called a Tax ID Number). You can apply for that EIN online, and you'll use this number to identify yourself as an officially formed business.

- When you create an LLC, you'll be required to create simple "articles of incorporation" to list your address and a registered "point of contact" person. You'll also need to create an "Operating agreement" which basically states who owns what. If you have multiple shop owners, this will require you to designate ownership (e.g., 50/50 or 60/40. This influences how much claim each of you will have on the business should you part ways.

- Creating an EIN will allow you to fill out a Sales Tax Resale or Exemption form, which gives you a backstage pass to the best wholesale prices for your product components—no sales tax required. Basically, you'll be able to buy wholesale supplies for your business tax-free, since you'll be creating items with those supplies to sell (and you'll be charging sales tax on those items you sell).

- "Limited Liability" means that you personally (as the owner) can't be sued/your personal assets won't be put at risk if you accrue debts or get into other entanglements. We all like to hope that won't happen (I've never had any such issues) but you never know! And if you do run up against a problem, you'll want to know that your liability is limited to the assets of your business—not your personal assets.

- Filing your tax return for an LLC business is really simple. An LLC doesn't actually require a return. You simply report your income and profit/loss from the business on your personal tax return as Schedule C income.

Summed up: Creating an LLC is easy, makes you look way more official, and protects your assets from potential legal situations. It also gives you the opportunity to get the best wholesale prices. DO it!

Whether or not you have an LLC, you're going to be paying both income tax (usually around 15%) PLUS self-employment taxes (usually around 15%) for a grand total of 30% in taxes. That's a frustratingly high rate. But as a self-employed person, the government requires you to pay that self-employment tax on TOP of your income taxes to account for medicare and social security (usually paid by an employer). Which brings us to our next section and arguably the most important reason to form an LLC as soon as possible in your Etsy journey.

What about S-Corps?

If your business takes off and you start thinking to yourself, "Maybe I could do this thing full time," you may want to apply to file your business taxes as an S-corp. You'll still be an LLC. But you'll file as an S-corp. I know that's confusing. But a lot of things about taxes and business entity stuff is. Just roll with it. I'll keep explaining.

S-corps are considered a "Pass-through" entity, which means that you'll be able to classify some of your earnings as "salary" (subject to employment taxes like medicare, medicaid, social security, federal withholding tax, etc.) and some as "distributions" (ONLY subject to income tax). You'll basically become a W2 employee of your own company, and you'll ONLY be required to pay employment taxes on the amounts you pay yourself as a salary. Put simply, as a self-employed person with an LLC, you'll pay around 30% in taxes on everything you make. If you file as an S-corp, you'll pay 30% in taxes ONLY on your "salary" and then just 15% in taxes on your "distributions."

Be aware that the IRS will scrutinize your business a little more carefully if you choose this designation, so most of the time you'll want an accountant's help in filing your yearly business taxes to make sure you're crossing your t's and dotting your i's.

The process of setting your business up as an S-corp is a matter of jumping through a bunch of bureaucratic hoops and red tape. It's a pain. And it's a learning curve to figure out which payroll tax forms you need to file yearly and quarterly (you must run payroll at least quarterly as an LLC filing as an S-corp), but I'm here to tell you that it's worth it when your business starts growing. Because it will save you a LOT in taxes. So find an accountant you trust, do the paperwork, and file as an S-corp once your business begins to grow and you're seeing regular income from your Etsy shop.

Setting Your Salary as an S-Corp

One of the biggest questions many people have about filing as an S-corp is how to determine the "salary" they'll pay themselves each quarter in payroll. The trick is to set a salary for yourself that is reasonable *for your business.* And when it comes to Etsy shops owners, that salary can be quite low. As in, your "salary" might only be a couple thousand dollars per year (or $500 per quarter) depending on the success of your shop.

I'm not an accountant. So, I'm going to remind you to get an ACTUAL accountant to help you navigate the process of filing as an S-corp. But I can tell you from personal experience that filing as an S-corp has saved me a lot of money in taxes and was absolutely worth the initial minefield of paperwork to get myself set up.

So, here's what filing as an S-corp functionally looks like for me each quarter during every three month period of the year (so Jan-March is Quarter 1, April-June is Quarter 2, July-September is Quarter 3, and October-December is Quarter 4):

- In month one and two, I pay myself a "distribution" or "draw." This draw isn't subject to any self-employment taxes. Just a straight 15% income tax. In March I run payroll for myself (because remember, I'm a W-2 employee of my company). I pay myself a quarter of my yearly salary, then pay a set percentage of that amount in taxes to medicare, social security, and tax withholding on EFTPS. (EFTPS is the government's online tax collection website, and you need to apply for an online account once you've been approved to file as an S-corp).

- Each quarter after running payroll for myself, I fill out a physical 941 form and send it to the IRS. I also pay a set amount in State withholding tax (to the state of Idaho in my case) and fill out form 910 online (you'll need to determine how much you pay in state withholding each quarter with your accountant).

- At the end of each year, I file 1099s for any contractors to whom I paid more than $500 over the course of the year, issue a W2 tax form for myself, mail in a FUTA form with payment (Annual Federal Unemployment Tax, so really it should be AFUT but I guess that sounded stupider than FUTA), file form 967 with my state to report my W2 and 1099 filings, and turn everything over to my accountant for taxes. Sounds like a lot, right? It WILL take you some time. It's a yearly task I don't relish any more than I relish my annual OB-GYN appointment.

But it's a huge improvement over paying a straight 30% in taxes. And all things considered, it's not really that bad.

BUT (and this is important, because remember, I'm NOT an accountant) you will probably need some ongoing support from an accountant who can answer questions about all the tiny, badly phrased, and cryptic boxes on all those tax forms, and so on. Which brings us to our next section: Accounting!

Let's Talk Accounting

Deep breath: Accounting. No matter what business designation you choose, or how little/much money your Etsy shop brings in, you are going to have some expenses and some income (e.g., the price of your product components, the price of equipment, and the earnings you bring in from Etsy and other venues).

The VERY first thing I want you to do is to open a business bank account. Even if your business is not very big yet. Mixing business and personal funds is a recipe for confusion and potential disaster if you get audited by the IRS. Just open a business account (it should be free to open a basic business checking account). Your business checking account will come with a corresponding debit card, and I recommend you apply for a business credit card (that you pay off every month and gives you some fun perks like travel rewards). Again, the business account is free, and it'll help you a lot. Even if your account balance is 50 bucks, just do it.

If you're just getting started (and electing to be an LLC instead of an LLC that files as an S-corp) you don't need to get an accountant yet, necessarily. I'd recommend it if you can afford it, but it's not strictly necessary. But here's the thing I didn't realize when I very first got started: whether you have an accountant or not, you DO need to do accounting. Here's the big to-dos if you're doing your own accounting:

Expense Tracking

Expense tracking is pretty much covering your butt come tax time. You're assigning categories to the business expenses you make (whether by check, cash, credit card, etc.) to indicate why those expenses were necessary for your business to operate, e.g., you're classifying the wooden dowels you purchased as "cost of goods sold" because you used those dowels to create arms and legs for the handmade dolls you sell on Etsy. Or the paper you bought as "office supplies" because you used it to print out fliers for an art show. You're telling the IRS, in general terms, what different expenses are for (because it's not always obvious).

You'll need to use an expense-tracking or general accounting app for this (I mean, you can do it with pen and paper or an Excel spreadsheet but it's going to be the end of your sanity).

The beauty of an expense-tracking program is that it directly connects to your business bank account, debit and credit cards to pull in every transaction. Then all you have to do is open the program and categorize each expense (e.g., "Office Supplies" or "Rent" or "Cost of Goods Sold" or "Payroll Taxes." The different categories available to you are the same categories that your accountant will use to determine how much you're liable for in taxes at the end of the year (e.g., some expenses are totally tax deductible, some are partially, and some aren't at all).

You'll have lots of options to choose from for expense tracking. The big names include Xero and Quickbooks. You'll have to pay a monthly fee for them, which is a bummer, but I personally like using Xero because my accountant is familiar with it and can jump in/see all my work easily. You'll also find free (generally simpler) apps. Make sure you look into pricing BEFORE you choose an expense tracking/accounting app. Because sometimes a "free" app may have hidden costs, e.g, it will only let you track a certain number of expenses per month before forcing you to upgrade.

Invoicing and Time Tracking

These are two separate logistical pieces of the business puzzle. But I'm grouping them together here because they dovetail well, and it'll make your life a lot easier.

You'll need invoicing for two reasons: To get paid by clients you complete work for, and to pay freelancers or employees you hire either on a regular basis or periodically for gigs. Using a time tracking/invoicing app helps everyone keep things straight. Because it's easy to think, "Oh yeah I'll remember I paid Jenny for that artwork…," but then in 3 months both of you are like, "Wait, did I pay her? How much?" Invoicing and time tracking provide a one-two punch of good record keeping for everyone's sanity. Time tracking will also help you gauge how long certain tasks take and will give you a better idea of whether it's worth your time to outsource different tasks or do them yourself as you grow.

Choose an invoicing program that also allows you to track time against different projects. Harvest and Time Tracking by Intuit are my favorites (they both offer a free "Self-Employed" option). Both apps have the option to track time against tasks and projects—either by pressing a "Start/Stop" button while working, or entering time manually. It's so, so easy to over/under estimate time—especially after the fact, when you've done 80 other things in between. Tracking hours with a simple app helps make sure you're staying accurate, keeping organized, and giving yourself the option to look at patterns and historical trends over time.

And the best part about time tracking software? When you're ready to create an invoice (either for payment or to pay a freelancer), you just select a project or client, click a button, and voila. An invoice is generated. It's great. No need to add up hours with a calculator or spreadsheet.

TIP: When you're invoicing for physical items instead of time (e.g., if you sell your mugs at wholesale prices to a retailer), I recommend using PayPal invoices. They have a simple-to-use invoice template for items (rather than hours). I don't typically send the invoices through PayPal, however (otherwise they'll charge you a percentage of your earnings). I tend to create draft invoices, print them as PDFs, and send them to my clients via email or in person.

Let's Talk Business Plans

You might not think you need a business plan. Especially if you're still growing. It sounds very official and intimidating and way too lofty of a project for little old you, who makes felted hats for American Girl Dolls in your kitchen by night. But I'm telling you, make a business plan. It can be really simple. And informal. But it will give you direction and help you hone in on your niche of the market on Etsy and zero in on the goals you have for your business and income.

All you have to do is open a Google doc and do the following (update this regularly, say once every six months to a year):

- **Write your business's elevator pitch:** Two sentences MAX that describe what you do and who you do it for. Why this is useful? This will allow you to clarify for yourself exactly who you are as a business, and to make sure you're occupying a niche of the market that is specific enough to be unique and compelling enough to draw buyers. It will also give you a ready answer when potential networking opportunities come your way, asking, "So what do you do?" I fumbled my way through enough replies before I wrote out an answer that I PROMISE you this is worth it. You sound confident, polished, and professional. And that's a really good thing. For example, your elevator pitch could be, "I hand-knit vintage-style clothing for American girl dolls." Or "I own an ecommerce shop that sells pop-culture mugs and hats."

- **Write a longer business summary:** This one can be a few paragraphs. Tell us the WHO, WHAT, WHERE, WHEN, and WHY of your business. Who is behind this business? What is it exactly that you're doing? Where does the magic happen? What makes you unique? How long have you been doing this? And most importantly of all, WHY are you doing this? This information can be pulled when you're inevitably asked for a bio along the way (whether in a farmer's market ad or in an article someone contacts you for. It happens more often that you'd think.)

- **Pin down your market and average customer:** It's okay if this is a guess at first. Write down who you think you're selling to in terms of age, lifestyle, gender, location, interests, etc. Anything that you think makes your buyers unique. This will help you in crafting ads, creating sponsored and targeted social media posts, and in honing the voice you use to speak to these customers.

- **Create a detailed outline of profit/loss and expenses:** You need to know how much you're making on a given item you sell before you can start running sales, offer wholesale prices, or even gage whether you can turn this side-gig of an Etsy shop into a full-time job. Get as granular as you can, and update this often as you add new expenses. (See Book 1 for more info on how to price your items.)

- **Marketing and sales approach:** How will people find out about your items? Here's where you brainstorm, create hypotheses, and come back to evaluate what's working well (so you can do more of it and expand on it). This could include items like "Etsy Organic Search" or "Etsy Reviews shared on social media" or "Paid Facebook ads." (We covered Marketing and Sales in Book 2.)

- **Plans for growth:** This is always the part of the plan that intimidates me the most, and I'm sure I'm not alone. But this is where you dream big. How big or small would you ultimately like to get? It's okay if you want to stay small. And it's okay if you have huge aspirations. Define what you want, and write out what the smaller steps in between might look like to get there.

Business Licenses and Permits

While you will need to register your business with your state as an LLC or an LLC that files as an S-corp, you won't necessarily need a **business license.** Check your state's requirements. Most have a "regulatory wizard" you can use to determine which hoops you have to jump through so that you won't get in trouble legally. Most of the different types of business licenses required are related to products in a certain field (e.g., agriculture). Many Etsy shop owners won't need a business license at all.

You will, however, need a **sales tax permit.** If you sell products (you almost certainly do if you sell on Etsy), you'll need to register your business as an entity that is legally allowed to withhold sales tax. You'll need to pay that sales tax to your state either monthly or yearly (make sure you plan on this expense and don't consider the sales tax you collect on Etsy as part of your "income.") And don't worry, Etsy automatically collects sales tax from your customers based on your state and requirements.

Deciding on a Business Location

Okay, enough logistics related to taxes and payroll. Let's talk about WHERE you are going to do your work, make your products, and operate your empire. This one can be stressful to figure out especially if you're in a growth phase. And Etsy shop owners often have unique needs for a location because of the unique products they make.

Still, there's some helpful rules of thumb you can follow to find a good fit. Start by addressing these topics:

- Whether you're selling online or primarily in person.

- Whether you're selling direct to customers (e.g., at a farmer's market) or wholesale (e.g., to other stores who markup and sell your products to their customers).

- How much revenue your business in consistently bringing in.

- How messy your production process is.

- How much space and equipment your production process requires.

- Your mental health and sanity (sometimes it's stressful to have messy, in-process stuff lying around in your personal space that might get knocked over or disrupted).

- The volume you're producing.

- Your goals for expansion.

The best location for your business will likely change as your business grows and develops. When I first started out, I was in the experimental phase and was making shirts for myself and a few friends. So I purchased minimal equipment and worked out of my basement closet.

When I grew a little more and built out my Etsy presence/started seeing more sales, I moved my operation into a whole room in the house. Then a garage. And finally a 700-sq ft. studio that I share with three other artists who don't need much space. I've grown a lot, but I've found that I can save a LOT on overhead by staying compact and making good use of my space.

Here's a few of the top places you might consider running your Etsy business, depending again on the factors above (like size and income) along with pros and cons.

- **A room (or part of a room) in your house/apartment:**

Pros: No additional overhead. You can deduct some of your utilities and home internet and phone from your taxes since those are business expenses too. Very accessible. You'll generally be home to arrange any customer drop-offs or pickups. Good temperature control.

Cons: Unless you have extra room, you might be edging in on your living space. Potential for projects and crafts to get disrupted. Your spouse or SO may object. Customers may need to pick up or drop off, which can sometimes be uncomfortable or awkward. Not a ton of space for bigger equipment. Depending on your production process, this can get messy or loud and may damage your carpet, sinks, or counters. May not be ideal ventilation if you use paint or products that produce VOCs.

- **Your garage (or an extra bay in your garage):**

Pros: No additional overhead. You can deduct some of your utilities and home internet and phone from your taxes. Very accessible. You'll generally be home to arrange any customer drop-offs or pickups. More space. Less concerns about mess or noise. Better ventilation if you use paint or products that produce VOCs.

Cons: You may be edging out a car or other storage. Potential for projects and crafts to get disrupted (or run over, or eaten by your dog). Your spouse or SO may object. Customers may need to pick up or drop off, which can sometimes be uncomfortable. Cold in the winter, and very hot in the summer. Insects like spiders and flies. Not always the most professional appearance to customers or others you want to impress.

- **A Co-op (an artist's co-op, or a shared maker space in your city):**

Pros: Less cost than renting an entire studio or warehouse. More space. No worries about making a mess in your own home. Ability to leave work for the day and keep your home a sanctuary. Good temperature control. Networking and social opportunities with other artists. Low risk, depending on your lease terms. Access to shared equipment like easels, sinks, break room and microwave, etc.

Cons: More monthly overhead. Not as accessible some of the time (may have restricted entry hours). Some restrictions on how you may use the space. Potential for projects and crafts to get disrupted or "borrowed" by other artists around your space who have access to your materials. Not a ton of space for bigger equipment. You might not be welcome if you use paint or products that produce VOCs. You may be responsible for some kinds of studio damage.

- **Your own leased studio or warehouse**

Pros: You can choose the amount of space you need. More possibilities for larger equipment and assembly areas. You determine hours and work environment. No worries about making a mess in your own home. Ability to leave work for the day and keep your home a sanctuary. Typically decent temperature control. Ability to sublease with other artists if you have more space than you need (this is what I do, to cut down on rent costs and enjoy some socializing and good vibes in the studio). Very accessible whenever you need it. Crafts and projects won't get disrupted. Better ventilation. You have the ability to create the environment and working space you desire.

Cons: Significant responsibility signing a long-term lease. More cost than a shared co-op. More monthly overhead. May still be some restrictions on how you may use the space. You may be responsible for some kinds of studio damage that would come out of your deposit.

Creating a Business Presence on LinkedIn, Google, Social Media, Etc.

When it comes to your business, the web can feel like an ever-expanding black hole that requires all of your attention and time. That's not entirely untrue. But just because you CAN spend all your time trying to keep track of and create a business presence in every corner of the web, but should you? Probably not. Like we said in Book 2 when we dug into different social media platforms, your time is valuable, and you should spend your time and effort where it's actually going to make a difference to your business.

As you look at where to establish a business presence, ask yourself, "Where do most people spend time networking, finding business help, and exploring?" And most people don't fly all over the web. They use the same handful of large, established platforms, which means you need to be present on those platforms—not everywhere. Here's where I recommend you create a business presence. It doesn't have to be fancy, just make sure you update it somewhat regularly.

LinkedIn

Everyone uses LinkedIn. It's the Facebook of business. It lends legitimacy and potential networking opportunities to your business. Create a business profile and update your personal profile to show that you are the owner of said business. Then spend an hour adding some beautiful photos and written descriptions to tell everyone what you do and where you're located (even if that's online). Not having a LinkedIn presence can make folks suspicious that you're fly-by-night or not very well established.

Google

Claim your business and create a profile for it on google. Not only will this allow people to review your business, but it will help you with visibility and may very well be the first thing that comes up in search (because, let's face it, everyone uses Google as their search engine). Keep your business hours and location accurate. If you work out of your home, there's no need to put your address, just list a website.

Facebook and Instagram

We already talked about tapping social media for paid ads and promotions in Book 2. But if that wasn't reason enough to put your business out there on social media (namely Facebook and Instagram, the heavy hitters), consider this: Facebook is the top social media platform that connects people (and businesses and ideas and events). You absolutely need a business Facebook page even if you think Facebook is dumb and you don't spend much time there personally. It helps people find you, it allows you to launch ads, it gives you the power to create events or quickly communicate information to your base of followers, and it allows people to discover you online in a way that highlights your personality and offerings (because you can share away!). Facebook helps legitimize your business as real and thriving. And there's no need to post to Facebook all the time, just enough to add value to your customers' lives, make them smile, and communicate important information.

Instagram can likewise generate a LOT of social capital for your business and even connect you to new opportunities locally for your business. In-person business opportunities, potential partners, potential workspaces, potential clients, and potential contractors will often peruse your social media accounts prior to deciding whether they want to work with you. So make sure you are reflecting your business well (and that you are findable!)

Things We Learned the Hard Way

Basically everything in this chapter was at one point hard for me. I thrive on creativity, and the nuts and bolts of starting a business made me feel dead inside.

That means I willfully ignored some aspects—like creating a business plan, taking the time to put my business on different important platforms, and finding the right fit for invoicing and time tracking. Don't be like me. It meant backtracking and frustration and missed opportunities that I later recognized. Do the boring, soul-killing stuff. Just do it. Most of this only has to be done once, and the earlier the better!

CHAPTER 2

Expanding and Scaling

CONGRATULATIONS AGAIN! YOU ARE GROWING! (Or you're reading this chapter in case you need to scale in the future, in which case, great job for being prepared and having the foresight and confidence that you CAN grow and succeed!)

My biggest advice on scaling is to spend 80% of your energy focused on the terrain coming up ahead—and 20% on the horizon: The place you're eventually headed. Big dreams are the result of little dreams falling into place through dedicated work and planning. And trying to force growth, or scale before you're ready, is going to result in wasted resources and misguided attention that needs to be spent elsewhere.

Basically, don't FORCE scaling. And don't get so focused on the horizon that you go off-road. But vice-versa, don't get so caught up on the rocky road that you forget where you're headed and why. What I mean is, work hard to facilitate growth and sales and achieve the smaller goals that will get you to your bigger goals (e.g., instead of focusing on 100% year over year growth, a great big-picture goal, focus on setting a goal to create a solid keyword strategy for five new listings each week). The biggest mistake I see from over-eager Etsy sellers is trying to artificially force growth before doing the work to reach those goals (e.g., by buying a larger studio space WAY earlier than needed or shelling out a lot of money for Kim Kardashian to promote your product when you have 53 Instagram followers). Take it easy. Celebrate the signs that you are growing (we'll talk about those next), and adjust your business as needed to grow.

Are You Ready to Scale? Evaluating Your Growth

Most of the time, you'll grow and scale little by little without even realizing it (that's a good thing, because scaling overnight is hard and stressful). Here's some positive signs that your business is growing:

- Your stats dashboard tells you so! Check it often. Look at your conversion rate, number of sales, and weekly/monthly visits. All of these things should be improving on a monthly and yearly level. Sometimes if you get too granular, it can look like something is wrong (e.g., day by day). But remember, the day of the week, the economic atmosphere, and the season all play key roles in whether or not people are shopping. Some fluctuation is normal, and growth isn't a straight line. But your overall trend should be upward.

- You find yourself buying in larger bulk amounts for supplies as you see consistent sales and positive trends.

- You're paying a LOT in taxes and it sucks (but hey, that means you're earning a lot)!

- You're spending more time on your Etsy shop (and seeing corresponding sales).

- You're bursting at the seams in your original space.

- You find yourself trying to streamline your processes to make them increasingly efficient and productive .

- You find yourself daydreaming of doing this job full time—and feeling like that might be a possibility based on your sales and traffic .

All of these are good indications that you're growing. In general, you don't need to worry that your sales are suddenly going to disappear overnight. Etsy rewards good sellers and good products with increased traffic and visibility. Just like it penalizes poor sellers and poor products with lower visibility. When you make money, Etsy makes money. That's a symbiotic relationship, my friend. So keep doing what you're doing, keep doing more of the things that seem to correlate with good reviews and more sales, and you can be pretty confident that you'll continue to grow.

Don't be afraid of growth, especially in areas where that growth creeps up on you. It can be easy to go on autopilot, for instance, and keep buying that 10-pack of envelopes when you should really be springing for the 100-pack (even though it's a more expensive upfront investment). Look at your growth trends and stats regularly, and use those trends to inform you of the risk level it's acceptable (and desirable) to take in improving your profit margins by purchasing in bulk, spending money on ads, etc. Always make sure your risk and expenses fall in line with your growth level. Being too conservative or too aggressive is not going to serve you in the end.

How to Scale: The Big Three

Again, if you're incorporating the advice in this book and spending consistent time on your shop and your product offering, I'm willing to bet that you are already scaling. Most of scaling is intuitive, and most growth you'll take in stride as you adapt and adjust to your business's changing needs. But there are a few key aspects of scaling that stump all of us: Primarily, moving into a dedicated workspace, changing your business structure, and hiring employees or freelancers.

We've already talked about the logistics of different business types in previous chapter, but how do you know you're ready to take the leap? It's one thing to order a REALLY BIG package of stamps. It's another to sign a year-long studio lease or make a foray into running payroll for the first time!

Let's talk about those three big aspects of scaling.

Making the Leap to a Dedicated Workspace

First of all, there is no rule that says you're only a "real" business if you have a brick and mortar presence, or a super cool decorated studio. Those things might be ideal, but it all depends on your business and how you make your products. Some people will NEVER need a dedicated studio space no matter how much they grow because the supplies and space they need to create their product are minimal, and they don't really interact with customers much outside of virtual spaces. If so, that's great. You are legit. Don't add extra expenses to your plate if you don't need them.

However, many Etsy shop owners may grow to the point where a shop, studio, or dedicated workspace is beneficial and will facilitate future growth (instead of stalling you out because of your space limitations).

Here's the top three signs that you should make the leap to a dedicated workspace:

- You consistently make enough sales that you can afford rent for a dedicated workspace. (This doesn't have to be a ton of money. Like we talked about in Book 2, a shared studio space can be surprisingly affordable.)

- Having more space would allow you to streamline and increase production, to bring in more sales (e.g., you purchase equipment that speeds up your process but doesn't fit in your current workspace).

- Your current workspace consistently creates logistical barriers to creating your products or interacting with customers.

Hiring Employees, Contractors, Consultants, and Virtual Assistants

Hiring ANY kind of contractor or employee can be very intimidating. I was so intimidated that I allowed myself to burn the midnight oil far longer than I should have because hiring and managing sounded so scary. I honestly should have hired someone part time much earlier.

But how will you know if you're ready to hire in any capacity? Part-time employees, consultants, and full-time employees are different options with benefits and drawbacks for each. For any hire you make, you should consider your needs, the type of commitment you can offer, and your budget.

When to Hire Consultants

You should consider hiring a consultant if you have a knowledge gap that's keeping you from doing something you want to do. In other words, when you need someone with more knowledge than you have to reveal some trade secrets—for a price—whether that's advertising, supply chain issues, design analysis, branding, etc. Hiring a consultant is basically hiring a very knowledgeable freelancer to step in and say, "Do this, stop doing that, here's why." Most consultants step in to impart knowledge, then step out of your business. They teach you to fish. The actual work of fishing is still up to you.

Be very careful who you hire as a consultant. The web is full of flashy gurus who claim that they can deliver the sun and moon. Ask for lots of recommendations before you commit to a consultant (especially for a high price tag), and set clear expectations of the type of interaction you'd like to have.

When to Hire Contractors or Virtual Assistants

A contractor or freelancer is someone who will help you with your business on an ongoing basis (this might be several hours per week, or once a month). You can find contractors available for hire on sites like freelancer.com, through networking on Etsy forums, or simply in your circles of friendship by asking for recommendations. When you feel yourself getting stretched thin as your business grows, or you identify a gap in ability or interest that you have (e.g., you want someone who can help you write copy or do design work because those just aren't skills you want to hone), a freelancer or contractor can help you take your shop to the next level and free up your time to focus on the big picture.

Choose someone you can trust who has the ability to work independently and think on their feet. Trust your instincts, and make sure you do a short Zoom interview (or an in-person interview if you're in the same city), and don't be afraid to walk away if it's not a good fit. It can be a good idea to do a "trial period" to make sure that you jive in terms of work and personality. Set clear expectations about what exactly you need, what your budget for contracting is, and how that contracting help will free up your time to run your business. Getting clear on these points yourself will help ensure a good relationship with freelancers. Answering these questions will also help you prioritize the type of work your contractor does in your Etsy shop.

Put your requests for work, prioritization, and any other tasks for your freelancers in writing, through email or google docs. Not only will this force you to nail down what you want your freelancer to do, but it will be a useful point of reference as you adjust workflows and tasks and can be very useful for a freelancer to reference.

You'll need to issue a 1099 form to any contractor who completes work in excess of $500 total throughout the year, come tax time. And make sure you order a PAPER form from the IRS well in advance of the tax deadline. Because the government has decided that's a hoop you'll need to jump through.

Basically, don't be afraid to hire freelancers, virtual assistants, or contractors in some capacity when you have the bandwidth to do so. Trying to do everything yourself might feel like the frugal or the easiest option, but if you're mired down in the details and trying to wear too many hats, it can make it very difficult to move forward in your business and grow. Give yourself some breathing room and bring on some help, in whatever capacity you need, as you are able.

Changing Your Business Structure

For most Etsy shop owners, the big question is whether or not to file as an S-corp. We've talked about the logistics of structuring your business, but how will you know when to make a change?

The short answer is, talk to your accountant. And if you don't have an accountant, find an accountant. Every situation is slightly different, but in general if your Etsy shop grows to the point where you're thinking of it as a very substantial part-time or full-time job, it's going to be important to look at your business structure and how to minimize your tax burden. I file as an S-corp, and honestly I wish I'd made that move sooner. It was a pain to make the switch but 100% worth it. TALK TO YOUR ACCOUNTANT.

Making the Leap to Full-Time Etsy Shop Owner

Deep breath. This is the dream that so many of us have. It's the dream I had when I started out on Etsy. And I still feel so happy that I've been able to achieve that goal.

So, I know this probably isn't what you want to hear: But I can't tell you when or if it's the right time to make the leap to full-time status.

I left a full-time, traditional corporate job to pursue my Etsy shop full time. And it was exciting, but it was also SCARY. I was giving up insurance benefits, a salary, and an office. But my Etsy shop was bursting at the seams (because of the very same strategies we've shared with you so far in this book!), and I had to make a choice. Either I was going to back away from my shop to keep it as a manageable side gig, or I was going to go full steam at it and quit my day job. I chose to quit my day job—after spending a lot of time with spreadsheets and budgets and worst-case scenarios.

Like many Etsy shop owners, I often take on work outside of my Etsy shop when the opportunity arises and it's a good fit. I also work as a freelance writer and consultant. This keeps me VERY busy, but it also gives me a bit more job security. If something happens on Etsy (like a market crash, a lull, whatever), I still have other sources of income. Making the leap to full-time Etsy can be significantly less scary if you do the same. Use your skill sets (I know you have MANY!) to branch out and freelance in other ways, whenever possible, to create multiple smaller streams of income as a safety net.

It's worth nothing that there's also nothing wrong with deciding to keep your Etsy habit small or as a permanent side gig. But if you want to pursue it as your career and your day job, it's absolutely possible and doable. If you have a good idea, are able to scale, and are seeing consistent sales by implementing the strategies in this book, the chances you'll succeed are quite high.

Thinking Like a CEO

So, is there something beyond a full-time job doing what you love? That all depends on your dreams, personality, and production process. Some Etsy shop owners who grow enough to make their hobby or passion as creators a full-time job find that they get burned out by running a full-time business. If that's you, it's time to start thinking like a CEO. Because, well, you are!

Which parts of your (thriving! Look at you go!) business do you love the most: Creating things? Social media? Which parts do you get burned out on: Marketing? Customer service? Now is your chance to redefine your role in your own company and business, and bring on others to help with growing pains, new needs, and skill-set gaps.

Some Etsy shop owners get discouraged when they finally realize their dream of running their Etsy shop full time and think, "Man, I hate some parts of this." Don't despair. And don't give up. YOU are in charge of your destiny here. It's your business. Make it work for you!

Things We Learned the Hard Way

There's no way around it: Scaling is hard and very individual work. It requires creativity and the ability to read signals from a lot of aspects of your business. Scaling also requires you to take an honest look at weak points in your business and to take some calculated risks as you grow.

Basically, it's kind of hard. And that's okay. Everyone does this the hard way. So don't be afraid to ask for help, pace yourself, and get creative. You don't have to grow in the same way everyone else does. In fact, I'd call *that* the biggest lesson in scaling that I learned the hard way: Trying to grow like everyone else. Every time I've gotten too caught up in some arbitrary benchmark of growth (like Instagram followers, for instance) it throws me off my game. Grow in the ways that make sense to you, at the pace that works for you. Don't be afraid to set goals or take calculated risks as you grow, but do so in a way that serves your business and you as a person. Because when you own an Etsy shop, you are your business.

CHAPTER 3

Shipping and Fulfillment

When my Etsy shop was really small, shipping was no problem. But as we've grown and this has become my full-time job, shipping is a little more complex. Which is why we've included this section here, after we've talked about growing and scaling your business.

Making a slew of sales is the shiny, fun side of the coin. Shipping and fulfillment is the "oh crap" on the flip side.

I understand. I was So. Bad. At shipping and fulfillment when I was in the awkward growth phase of my business. It was the bane of my existence when I really started to get the Etsy snowball rolling, bringing in enough sales to sustain me as a day job. Shipping and fulfillment was easy when I had two or three or ten or even twenty sales each week. But my exhilaration at seeing the sales numbers go up was dampened by the mess of shipping and fulfillment.

This wasn't all my fault. Back then, Etsy's tools weren't exactly made to accommodate larger shops or high-volume sales. They've come a long way, and so have I. In this chapter, we'll make sure you're all set to deliver on your promise of sending your products to your waiting customers efficiently and cost-effectively (and at SCALE!).

Shipping Timelines

Good shipping and fulfillment starts with good communication in setting realistic timelines. You have the option to choose one of Etsy's timeline options when you create your shipping profile (e.g., 1-day, 3-5 days, 1-2 weeks, etc.).

Faster is always better—as long as it's realistic. Especially since Etsy's algorithms reward you for faster shipping by allowing customers to sort listings by shipping speed! So, make sure you are shipping out your items regularly and as quickly as you can (while taking your capability, schedule, and production process into account. You'll only have upset customers and bad reviews if you over-promise and under-deliver).

You probably already know that once your buyer makes a purchase, the shipping countdown automatically begins for both you and them. You and your buyer can easily see the status of their order and whether or not it falls into the shipping timeframe you specified. A couple things to know:

- Again, your buyers can search for products based on shipping speed. And (unsurprisingly) they often choose to narrow their search based on short shipping timeframes. But like I said: Stay realistic. If your buyer expects a shipment within a day, there's typically a reason. A birthday, a Christmas present, a vacation, etc. If you don't make good on your end of the bargain, you're going to get bad reviews and frustrated convos.

- Holidays and weekends don't factor into your countdown. So, if you ship once a week on Mondays, you can choose 3-5 days as your shipping time frame, and even if a customer ordered over the weekend and their order doesn't come until the next Friday, that still counts as 3-5 *business* days.

- Update your timelines regularly. If you're sending out products more quickly (because you innovated or because you hired someone or whatever), don't forget to update your shipping time frames.

- Shipping in batches means fewer post office trips and the ability to "assembly line" your packaging process. I ship either once or twice per week, because it saves me a LOT of time by packaging everything up at once and hitting the post office just once.

Calculated Shipping

Take the time to weigh and measure your products, then input that information into Etsy. I know it's a pain. Do it anyway. Even if you sell a number of different variations of a product that weigh different amounts. I avoided doing this for a long time because it sounded like a huge pain. I sell t-shirts, and each size (I list sizes as multiple variations within a listing) weighs a different amount. An extra-small shirt weighs about 4 ounces, while a 3XL weighs about 9. But Etsy only allowed me to list one shipping weight for all the variations in the listing. So here's what I finally worked out:

1. The hours I was spending in the post office having each item weighed weren't worth the 50 cents I thought was saving per item by doing my own shipping. I should have made my life simple and estimated generously on my weights in Etsy.

2. In the end, the amount I saved by purchasing through Etsy (instead of retail at the post office) more than made up for any overly generous estimations.

To set up calculated shipping, I broke my listings down into categories by product type—with weight and size being the most significant factor. And then I weighed the heaviest and largest item in each category, e.g., my largest sweatshirts weighed 13 ounces. My largest t-shirts weighed 9 ounces. And my largest baby outfits weighed 3 ounces. I used the same packaging for all of them, so that was constant.

Then it was just a matter of inputting the maximum weight into each listing (depending on its product type) as well as the size of the product once it was ready to be packaged (make sure all dimensions are slightly smaller than your package preference sizes, or else Etsy will think your item won't fit in the package.

You'll need to make sure your packaging preferences correspond with your calculated listing dimensions and weights that you just input into each listing (e.g., if your item will fit in a 15-inch flat-rate envelope, make sure you list its length as less than 15 inches). Etsy automatically lists common package sizes, along with all of the flat rate packaging options offered by UPS and FedEx. You can also create custom package preferences that allow you to input the dimensions of the specific packaging you use along with any handling fees you want to tack on.

Carefully read through the different options in your Shipping Settings (within your Etsy Dashboard, go to Settings > Shipping Settings). These settings have the ability to save you lots of time. For instance, if you allow Etsy to fill out your customs forms, you won't have to spend time at the post office with those obnoxious forms. And if you allow Etsy to pre-fill your label information, all you'll have to do when printing labels is review them to make sure all the information looks correct.

Why I Recommend Using Etsy Shipping over Third-Party Apps

There are a number of integrations designed to make your shipping experience "seamless," like ShipStation. Some Etsy shop owners love these apps. I find it adds more hassle to my process than keeping everything in one place (Etsy), especially since Etsy and the post office have added more features recently that streamline the shipping and tracking process. Keeping everything within Etsy is simply less hassle and less back-and-forth. Not to mention, Etsy affords you many of the organizational features you'd get with apps like ShipStation for free (like discounts, tracking on every purchase, and the ability to refund a label right within the dashboard).

Purchasing labels through Etsy and USPS (or your country's national postal service) also mitigates any loss you might incur by overestimating on weight. For US customers, the post office now actually REFUNDS you if you overestimate on your package weight. That's right. Each week I now see an email stating that the post office has adjusted a number of my labels—refunding the difference to my Etsy account. So, don't worry too much about overestimating when you buy your labels in Etsy for USPS.

Using Etsy's Labels and Packing Slips

Again, I wholeheartedly recommend that you use Etsy's labels and packing slips.

Not only do you get around 15-30% off retail prices on shipping labels, but it saves you endless time at the post office and allows you to track every single package you send right from within Etsy.

Even better, as soon as you create a label within Etsy, it sends a notification to your buyer with their tracking number (saving you time answering questions about tracking).

As for physical labeling supplies, I get my physical labels from Amazon in bulk. (I buy half-sheet self-adhesive shipping labels.) You can also purchase labels in bulk from Uline.com and other paper wholesalers.

I don't include packing slips when I send orders to customers. (That information is so readily available in a customer's inbox), and so many people purchase their item as a gift that most don't want the packing slip included anyway. But I DO use a PDF print of these packing slips to tell me exactly what I should be putting in each customer's order.

Warning! If you frequently ship outside the country your shop is located, you may want to consider including packing slips AND invoices in your packages so that if customs opens your packages, they can see exactly what's in there and how much it's worth. This very rarely happens with Etsy parcels, but some sellers have had problems, so it's worth noting here.

Step-By-Step Instructions for Creating Labels and Packing Slips

Here's my process for printing **labels** (the thing you stick on your package) and **packing slips** (the list that shows what's in a customer's order and tells you what to put in their package) when I ship.

1.	First things first: Review your orders for any buyer notes or private notes you've added to remind yourself to update an address or name on any of the labels (more often than is convenient, you'll get messages from buyers who forgot to give you the correct shipping address). You'll also want to make a note for yourself of any orders that need two labels/need to be sent using two packages (e.g., if you're sending a greeting card and a T-shirt in separate packages so the card won't get bent).

2.	In your Etsy Dashboard, select all the orders you'd like to print labels for. Then hit the "Get Labels" button at the top of your orders.

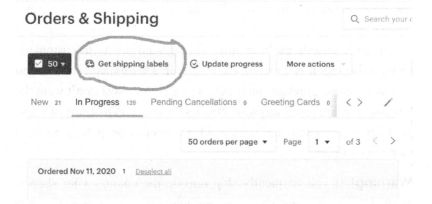

3.	Now, review for any problems/change any addresses you noted. Look for any red warning signals that an address isn't formatted correctly. (Sometimes people put in REALLY long names, and Etsy only allows a certain number of characters, so you'll need to shorten the names. I just do this as best I can.)

4.	Here's what the interface looks like when you're purchasing labels. Notice that Karen is first, followed by Amanda. When you are satisfied that all the addresses look good and are all correct, simply click "purchase."

5. Once you hit "purchase," a dialogue box will pop up that gives you a few different options including "Print shipping labels," "Print packing slips," and "Create a USPS SCAN form." DON'T CLOSE IT. First, choose "Print labels." Then print your physical labels using your printer.

6. Here's the PDF etsy generated for my package labels. Again, notice that Karen is first, followed by Amanda.

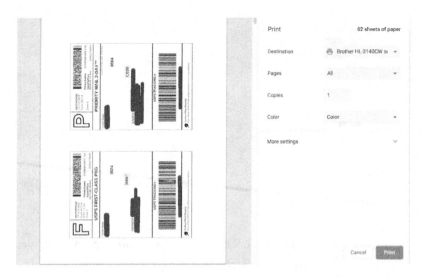

7. Now go back to that dialogue box and choose the option "Print Packing Slips." This will produce a PDF (complete with pictures!) of the order items that should go in each package. (You can print this to include in each package if you want!)

8. Here's what the first page of my packing slips look like. Again, notice that Karen is first. These packing slips (that tell me what to put in each package) correspond with the order of the shipping labels I just printed to place on each package. Now I can stuff packages in order.

Basically, if you have 124 open orders (like I do here) you'll now have 124-pages of packing slips that show you exactly what to put in each package. The order of your shipping labels will correspond with the order of your packing slips. As you affix each label to your mailers or packages, simply refer to your handy packing sheet. This process makes packing up products a breeze. You'd be surprised how easy it is to mix up packages and customer names (e.g., put Karen's order into Amanda's package) when you're packing everything up. Keeping your packing list and labels in the same order makes for one less headache. This becomes more and more important the more orders you have coming in.

TIP: A USPS SCAN form allows the USPS to scan all your packages in one push of the button. It's a very handy feature, but you will need to print out a form for the post office—and you won't be able to do so if you're printing your labels to ship at a future date (Etsy allows you to print labels up to two days in advance of your mailing date). So usually I save time printing and just let USPS scan my packages. Sorry USPS.

Supplies for Packaging

Let's talk about the packaging you'll use to send your items. There's a few ways you can make sure your packaging logistics support your scaling efforts. Start by asking yourself the following questions:

1. Will this packaging keep my product safe enough to withstand the journey through the postal system?

2. Is this packaging the most cost-effective way to send my items? For US shops, usually USPS is your cheapest bet. I use them almost exclusively. They're fast, inexpensive, and reliable. Wherever you sell, your national postal service is also likely (but not guaranteed) to be your cheapest, most reliable option.

3. What types of packaging do I need to ship my products? Purchase this packaging in bulk (as long as you have a proven product). If you're still testing a new product's viability, it's probably worth it to pay more per piece for a small amount of

packaging so you aren't left with a pile of boxes that go nowhere. For small and mid-sized shops, Amazon has quite a bit of well-priced bulk packaging supplies. If you get really big, wholesale shipping suppliers like Uline have even deeper discounts.

4.   Within parameters 1-3, choose something fun that will make your buyer smile. Most of the time, there's no need to choose brown paper. Opt for something with donuts or unicorns or choose fuchsia pink instead of manila. This typically won't cost you much more, but it will make an impression on your buyer (we talk more about aligning your labels and packaging with your branding in Book 1).

Using Progress Steps to Stay Organized

Etsy allows you to create "progress" categories to keep yourself organized. USE THEM. Here's my process. (You should feel free to create your own categories depending on your unique creation process. You can create several different categories and name them whatever you'd like!):

•   All your incoming orders will automatically go into your "New" category. While you can create as many "progress" steps as you want, I prefer to keep things simple and divide my orders up into "New" "In Progress" "Pending Cancellations" (there's a delay between when you cancel an order and when Etsy removes it from your "New" orders, so I don't want to get mixed up and fulfill a canceled order) and "Greeting Cards" (since I treat this type of packaging differently).

- You should choose names that mirror your process of creation and fulfillment. Here's my process and how I use progress steps:

  o   As soon as I start working on a group of orders (ordering the supplies I need to create them, actively working on fulfilling them, etc.) I move them into the "In Progress" step. Later, when I'm ready to ship these orders I simply select everything in my "In Progress" tab and print those labels/packing sheets.

  o   It takes a while for Etsy to process cancellations. So I created a step especially for pending cancellations so that I don't accidentally start making those orders/they're out of sight, out of mind until they disappear/are fully canceled.

  o   Sometimes, when I'm testing a new product or just don't have the capacity to make it on my own, I drop ship (we'll talk about that more later in this book). I group these orders together so I don't worry about them. I check my drop shipping account once per week to verify that they've been sent out by my drop shipper, then mark them as shipped in Etsy.

  o   For products that I ship more frequently (like Greeting Cards) I create a "Misc" step so that I can select all the orders I'd like to send out that day, plop them into the

Misc category so I can easily see them all, and then send them out. The way you use steps will depend on your product and how often you ship, which brings us to our next section.

Shipping Frequency

I know we already covered shipping timelines—that's what you communicate to your buyer. Now let's talk about frequency—that's how often you *actually send out products*. I know some sellers that are packaging and shipping every single day. That works for some people, especially when you have a product you can package up and prep for shipping ahead of time or in bulk. Then it might make sense for you to ship every day.

However, for most sellers, the process of packaging and shipping is a bit onerous and takes a while. In that case, consider the assembly line philosophy. Onerous tasks with lots of moving parts are usually more efficient when you can group tasks together. Sending out five orders each day over five days is usually less efficient than sending out twenty-five orders in one day when you consider the time it takes to gather supplies, set everything out, go to the post office, arrange for a pickup, mark things shipped in Etsy and purchase labels, etc. That's why I ship once per week. I find it saves me the most time without allowing orders to build up too much. You'll want to find your own frequency, but be sure to consider efficiency and your sanity when doing so—not just your sales.

Using Order Notes to Stay Organized

Sometimes being an Etsy shop owner feels like one big game of concentration: There's a lot of moving parts, a lot of convos coming your way, and a lot to remember.

I stay organized (and sane) by using **Etsy's private notes** to remind me of anything important that comes my way in a convo. When you click on an order, Etsy opens a pop-up with details about that order and gives you the option to "add a private note" that only you can see. If someone needs an address change, I make an order note. If someone is anxious about arrival time and I decide to bump their shipping up to priority as a courtesy, I make an order note. If someone has been a huge arsehole and I want to include an extra goodie to make them feel warm and fuzzy inside when they open their package, I include an order note. Your buyer can't see these order notes, but they're easily scannable as you're looking through your orders.

I scan for order notes before I print labels (to look for address changes), before I purchase components for my products (in case someone changed a size or color on me), and while I package my products. It takes five minutes to scan even several pages of orders, and it allows me to stay supremely organized without a ton of effort on my part.

Basically, order notes are there for YOU (your customers can't see them), so use them to remind yourself of anything that will improve your workflow or customer service when fulfilling your orders. And scan often!

Warning: Private order notes DO show up on your packing slips when you print them, so if you include these in your packages, you'll probably want to delete "notes to yourself" so customers don't see them.

Stuff We Learned the Hard Way

I've done so many things wrong when it comes to packaging and shipping. And the stuff I do now seems like a "duh" when I look at my process and how well it works, but in the beginning I made a lot of mistakes. Here's the biggest ones:

Overly elaborate packaging: When I first got started selling on Etsy, I got intimidated looking at other sellers' packaging. I once ordered a shirt that was carefully wrapped in tissue paper, included five different free decals, was tied together with a sweet little twine bow, and included a heartfelt note. While this was beautiful and lovely, it didn't encourage me to make a repeat purchase, because the shirt didn't really fit me very well. Still, for a while I tried to make my packages very fancy and heartwarming. And then I got tired and overcorrected to very boring basic packaging. And guess what? My sales didn't suffer. I didn't get as many awesome reviews specifically praising my packaging—but I didn't get negative reviews about my packaging either. I finally found that a balance of EASY fun packaging was just as effective (and MUCH more efficient) than the super special packaging with cutesy wrapping. Value your time, and focus on what matters.

Hand-writing addresses and waiting in line at the post office: While I was still getting started—and even when I started to really grow—I hand wrote addresses on packaging. Finding the right labels sounded difficult, inputting the right information for calculated shipping sounded difficult, and the unknown was off-putting. So I wrote out my labels by hand and dutifully carried everything to the post office each week. Not only did I overpay by doing this, but I wasted WAY too much time. Do you know how long it takes to write out a bunch of addresses without making mistakes? A LOT OF TIME. And nobody got automatic tracking emails. Learn from my wasted time and inefficiency. Take the time to figure out calculated shipping and labeling. You will thank me, especially when the holidays hit.

Not keeping a strict order: Before I learned the trick of printing labels and packing slips at the SAME time (and in the SAME order), I wasted lots of time Control+F searching for names on my Etsy orders to match up labels with packing items. Don't do this. Not only was it more time consuming, but it resulted in regular errors as my eyes glazed over and I put Susan's shirt into Marianne's package because my brain got tired of doing the extra busy work.

The Bottom Line: Shipping and fulfillment doesn't have to be a nightmare or the dark side of making sales. If you're willing to put in a bit of time on the front end by using calculated shipping and Etsy's labels, you're going to find that packaging and fulfillment gets to be very streamlined and even easy. Don't go crazy with the packaging, but make it your own in easy and creative ways. Keep it simple, keep it accurate, and keep it organized.

CHAPTER 4

Supply Chain and Product Quality

Just like shipping and packaging, your supply chain (where you get the stuff to make and ship your products) and product quality (how well your product is made), are often put at risk by growth and scaling.

And we don't want that. We want to make sure that you can scale efficiently and cost-effectively—and that your products don't suffer.

By this point in the book it should be very clear, but it's worth repeating that WHERE you get the materials to hand-make your Etsy products is really important. Those beautiful, handmade products you create and send out into the world are only as good as your supplies. And the profits you bring in depend on the cost of those supplies. Basically, your income and your customer satisfaction depend heavily on your ability to source quality supplies at a great price. And at scale.

Whether you're just getting started or ESPECIALLY if you're expanding, it's important to understand a few important aspects of the supply chain (where you get your supplies). Because where you get the raw materials to make your products—and how good that final product actually is compared to what your customer expects and your competition's offerings—will have a direct impact on your reviews, sales potential, and profit margins. And ensuring that you continue to focus on your supply chain and quality as you scale will position you for sustainable growth instead of popping at the seams!

Supply Chain: Where to Source Your Stuff

For most people who create handmade goods, there are basically five places you can source your stuff. I use all five, depending on my needs and as I've grown. Now that I run my shop full-time, I rely more on wholesalers and bulk Amazon purchases, but I still use the other places on this list when I need a small quantity of something or am in a pinch.

- **Craft or office supply stores:** This is a great place to get small amounts of an item you use very infrequently or to create and test new products without investing a lot of money in bulk supplies. Craft shops tend to be reasonably priced, and you can usually find coupons. They're also useful in a pinch (e.g., you suddenly run out of adhesive or buttons and don't have time to reorder in bulk). Like we'll talk about in just a bit, it's not a great idea to buy stuff in bulk when you have an untested product or aren't really sure how much volume you'll be selling. Even if you're sure you have a great idea, iterate small until you prove yourself right. Craft and office supply stores are a great place to get the supplies to test ideas and find resources in a pinch.

- **Other Etsy shops:** Whether you're looking for bulk supplies, just a few supplies, or a particular kind of supply or material that you're having a difficult time sourcing, turn to Etsy. It's surprising how often this is a last resort for Etsy sellers. Turning to your fellow Etsypreneurs for your supplies can often help you find exactly what you need, at a great price, in either bulk or small quantities. If you find something close to what you're searching for but not exactly, there's also a good chance that you can request a custom product or component (a huge perk not available in most stores!). Rely on other artists to help you shine in an area they specialize without having to learn all the ropes yourself. For instance, I tried creating my own photo templates of apparel photos (photographing a blank t-shirt so I could photoshop my designs onto it later) with middling success for some time. But then I realized there were already people on Etsy doing the work for me—at a fraction of the cost (when I considered my time and subpar results). So now I purchase many of my blank apparel mockups from Etsy sellers who specialize in just that.

- **Amazon.com:** Amazon has a huge array of office products and some craft components that can be purchased in either smaller or bulk quantities. You'll typically find prices that are more competitive than Staples or other office supply stores, and it's easy to compare prices. I tend to use Amazon for my paper, office supplies, and other relatively boring things that I need to keep my business running.

- **Wholesale print shops:** For sourcing tags, business cards, and other marketing materials you may want to print, there's a good variety of wholesale printing presses online. Printrunner.com is my personal favorite. It's not as flashy as VistaPrint, and it won't hold your hand through the process, but it's straightforward and fabulously priced when you buy in bulk. I get my stickers and tags there. If you sell printed products like greeting cards or wall prints, you'll likely find that when you factor in the cost of good ink, a good printer, and good paper, it's actually cheaper to have someone else print your stuff in bulk.

- **Specialized wholesalers:** Since I print t-shirts, blank tees are the bread and butter of my business. Whatever the bread and butter of your business might be, find a wholesaler that offers exactly what you need and has the ability to sell it to you inexpensively and ship it to you in a timely manner. There's likely several options, so do your due diligence and price out wholesale options. Let them know you're shopping around, and ask about even deeper discounts as you establish yourself as a repeat customer with volume. As a general rule of thumb, if a wholesaler offers its prices to the public without requiring you to input your EIN (Employer ID Number) and business information to verify that you are indeed a business looking to buy wholesale (instead of a direct customer trying to score a few cheap items), you aren't going to get the best prices.

How to Know if You're Getting a Good Deal on Your Supplies

There are a few indications that you're getting a good deal on the supplies to create your product. As you grow and are able to scale, your margins should generally increase in a healthy way because you can justify buying more bulk supplies at a lower per-item cost. However, you may choose to narrow your margins to outpace your competitors and sell more items instead. The strategy is up to you, but what should be trending down at all times is your *cost per item* as you grow. If your costs are staying flat or increasing, take a careful look at your process, your supplies, and your fixed costs.

Here's a few questions to ask yourself when you evaluate your supply costs:

1. When you consider the cost of your time (e.g., if you can make 4 products in one hour, and feel good about making $20 per hour, mark that as $5 per product time cost) plus the cost of your supplies (including packaging, labels, and materials), how comfortable are your margins? Are you able to replace or resend a product (e.g., if it's damaged in shipping or not quite up to snuff) and still come out ahead? If not, it's time to take a hard look at your process for creating your goods, the cost of your supplies, or your retail price. We talked about how to price items in Book 1.

2. Have you done your homework and compared different wholesaler prices, asked about discounts for repeat and proven customers, and consistently find that you're getting the best deal for your needs?

3.   Are you buying in bulk where it makes sense to save money when you have consistent needs and proven sales potential? You can always expect deeper discounts for larger bulk orders, but sometimes spending a lot upfront to score a better price per item is going to put a strain on your business or doesn't make sense because you have a new product or idea that has yet to be evaluated in terms of sales potential. You'll need to evaluate the health of your business and establish sales potential (while accepting smaller margins) before you spring for those bigger bulk purchases. Because here's the thing: If you get 800 popsicle sticks for five cents a piece (instead of buying a conservative 80 popsicle sticks for ten cents a piece) and then don't use the majority of those popsicle sticks, it doesn't really matter that they cost five cents apiece because you won't be able to recoup your costs without *sales*. So you'll just be out $40 instead of $8.

4.   Are you able to offer similar pricing or undercut competitors' pricing because you've been savvy about how you purchase your materials and spend your time, without sacrificing product quality?

How to Verify the Quality of Your Components and Products

Maybe this is super obvious to some of you, but in case it isn't, let's talk about how you measure quality. It's not a completely objective process. Some people hate what other people love. But if you know your audience and your market, you should have a very strong sense of what MOST of your audience prefers. You won't be able to please everyone. But your goal should be to earn an A+ approval rating in impressing the vast majority (of your target audience, that is). Here's how you do that:

•   **You enjoy using your own product:** If you don't find yourself using it or feel hesitation about wearing it/putting it into your kids' hands, displaying it in your house, those are huge warning signs. If it breaks quickly or starts to look shabby after washing, you have a problem (unless that's what it's supposed to do).

- **Handmade tends to be synonymous with one of two things:** Superior quality and workmanship, or deeply inferior quality and workmanship. I'm sure you can guess which one you'd like to be associated with your brand. Etsy is all about the high-quality handmade. Which means that your shop will be held to a higher standard in many ways than products that appear to be mass-produced and sold on Amazon. That might seem a little unfair, but for better or worse that's the general consensus.

- **If your product wasn't designed for you (e.g., if you're a man, and women use your products primarily or vice versa) do NOT neglect market research:** You'd be surprised by how much reliable information you can gain from even a small audience (as long as it's the right audience). Don't guess. Don't assume. Don't ask a friend or your spouse. Give your product to strangers who don't have a stake in pleasing you with their answer, and find out what they hate about it and what they love about it.

- **Shop around, and don't settle:** You'll usually have a number of options for product components. Don't purchase until you find one you really, really like. You'll thank yourself later when you get those sweet reviews.

- **Listen to your negative reviews:** Yeah, negative reviews are painful. But do you want to know what's even more painful? Numerous studies have shown that for every person that takes the time to leave you a negative review, there's about 10 other people who stay silent but think the same thing. They just won't buy from you again, and studies show they'll probably steer their friends and acquaintances away from you without your knowledge ("The Secret Ratio That Proves Why Customer Reviews Are So Important," Inc.com).

Iterating Small with New Product Launches, (e.g., Testing the Market BEFORE Buying Bulk Supplies)

I've mentioned this in other chapters, but we're going to sit down and have a solid chat right now about testing the market and iterating small when you create new products to sell. Because too many Etsy sellers, once they taste a little success, will go nuts creating new products and listings in an attempt to snowball and grow faster.

But that's not usually a good plan of action. If you create a new or different product, it's better to start off slow, wait for the good signals from the market, and THEN proceed by buying supplies in bulk and going wild with advertising. Just remember: One success does not guarantee another success. And one successful product does not guarantee another successful product. It's a good start and a good launch point, but you should ALWAYS create a "minimum viable product" to launch new items in your shop. This is the most basic version of the product with the most minimal cost to you, to test the market's response. If you get good signals, then you're off to the races! If you don't, you've avoided spending a lot on sunk costs.

The following are some best practices to determine viability of new products. Now, if you're just getting started on Etsy, some of the information in this chapter might sound a little overwhelming. That's okay. Start where you're at, and use the ideas that make sense for your shop and situation; however, even if you're just getting started, you can test the market in easy ways to avoid the work of putting a bunch of dud products out there on Etsy.

The most important thing that new or established Etsy shop owners can do is to use data, not hunches, to decide which products you'll put in your shop or create. That's very important with any aspect of your shop, but especially costly new product launches.

Both new and established Etsy shop owners can make the mistake of putting a lot of work into "hunches" for good ideas about new products. If you're a new shop owner, you don't necessarily know what will sell yet. As a more established shop owner, you might not be aware of all the factors that go into whether a product is selling or not. Even if a product seems very similar to one you've released successfully, the small factors that make it different can tip the scales in a way you don't expect.

I find that Etsy shop owners who have seen some initial success are actually most vulnerable to creating new products based on hunches. Why? Because as you build your shop, get into a groove in sourcing your components and products, and start to see some success, it's easy to get overconfident and think your ideas are golden. While delightful and fun, this can make you overly confident when testing out new products and ideas and making purchasing decisions.

The Value of Research

So, how exactly does one gather data and research the chances of success on Etsy? First let the keywords guide your path. (You can review SEO and keywords in Book 1!)

Remember, you're ideally looking for those golden high- to mid-volume keywords with low- to mid-volume competition. Tools like eRank.com and Marmalead.com can help you identify those keywords. The goal, especially if you're just getting started, is to send quality, beautifully presented products out into the Etsy universe that won't get completely lost in the melee of competition. And you need to know that people are searching for those products. Because even the most beautiful, high-quality product won't sell much if nobody is looking for it. So, when you get a hunch for an amazing product, check your instincts by doing a little research into keyword volume and competition.

The Value of Iterating Small

Even if you've identified the perfect keywords, ecommerce can still ride on a lot of variables. So, whether you're new or established, you should always start small with a viable test to plumb the market and your audience, e.g., don't make 1,000 snakeskin wristlets in preparation for your golden idea. Instead, make one or two and see what happens.

Be willing to forgo a "great deal" on bulk supplies or the appeal of shaving a few more cents or dollars from your profit margins to take a risk. More often than not it will bite you in the butt. Why? Because whether or not a product sells can hinge on some subtle and mysterious factors—including imagery, marketing, advertising, quality, color, season, and even what happened that week in the news.

Protect your shop and your investment by keeping the jury out on new ideas or products until you've tested them. This can be done in a few ways:

- Put out a "limited offering" to encourage interested customers to purchase while supplies last and allow you to gage interest quickly.

- Outsource production of the new idea or product with a production partner (more on that next) who is already set up to make this product and is willing to let you buy smaller quantities. Your margins might be small, but you won't be stuck with a bunch of products you can't sell.

- If the product can be made or put together quickly, try creating a mockup or realistic image of what that product will look like, and advertising it BEFORE you purchase the components to gage interest. If you see lots of positive feedback and a few sales, that's a good indication you have a winning idea. If you get crickets, you can send me a thank you note.

- Create a small Facebook group or email list of repeat customers that have given you positive reviews on similar products and serve as "beta testers." These beta testers offer honest feedback and stay on your list, in exchange for a free product once in a while as a thank you.

Drop shipping and Production Partners

Do you have to make everything yourself because you sell on Etsy in a handmade marketplace? Nope. But you do need to be upfront about that fact and work with production partners and drop shippers selectively. Because at the end of the day, it's you who will be on the hook for customers with bad reviews or complaints that can hurt your shop. Let's start with a couple of definitions.

Drop shipper: Someone who produces a product for you and ships it to customers as if the product has come directly from you. Some Etsy owners use drop shippers exclusively, especially those who create apparel and accessories like bags and iPhone cases. Basically, a customer will buy the product from you, you give the order (and the customer's address) to the drop shipper, and the drop shipper sends the item to the customer (with your return address on the label). A good drop shipper is invisible. Your customer shouldn't ever know they exist (unless they look at the information on your listings about production partners, since you have to disclose this information).

Pros of using drop shipping

The biggest appeal of drop shipping is that it's easy. Some platforms like Printful.com are even quite streamlined and automated, so you can actually integrate your Etsy shop and fulfill orders automatically whenever one comes in. This can be a great way to test the validity of a new product or a new Etsy shop without investing a ton in your own equipment or production space. Drop shipping can also be a good way to test out new product ideas without fully committing. You can use drop shipping to sell items your customers might love that you aren't interested in making yourself (like iPhone cases, for instance).

Cons of using drop shipping

If something goes wrong, your margins are so small that you're probably going to lose money on the sale (unless it was the drop shipper's fault, but even then you might have a very annoyed customer on your hands who just wants a refund instead of a replacement). Not to mention the pride factor. Some customers want stuff made by YOU and feel a little annoyed if (after reading your awesome "about" story) they notice you're using a drop shipper to create your products.

TIP: Spend some time really getting familiar with drop shipping. Because an "oops" on your end, (e.g., selecting the wrong brand of shirt to send out) is a much more costly mistake than if you had produced that product on your own. If you have to send out a replacement, you'll likely lose money on the order. You'll also want to make VERY sure that any images you upload are high-resolution and don't contain barely-visible stray pixels. I've made that mistake a couple of times, and I've had to send out a replacement when my customer got a shirt with a little pixel splotch on it (which was totally my fault). Double and triple check ALL your work when you drop ship.

Production partner: A production partner helps you make your product (rather than making the entire thing). There's a bit of gray area here, since you're not required to list EVERY product component you include as a production partner. However, if a hefty portion of your product is made or created by someone else, list your production partner (you'll have the opportunity to explain your relationship with that production partner in a blurb when you list them as a partner on Etsy).

For instance, if you sell earrings in your shop that are primarily concepted and created by someone else (but you package them up and maybe add your own special touch to the ear wire) that shop or person should be listed as a production partner. However, if you use felt or linen for sewing projects, you don't need to list the fabric store as a production partner. It's all in how much of a role that partner plays in creating the *finished product* that your customer buys. Etsy wants its customers to have transparency in sourcing and creation. People feel betrayed when they think they're buying hand-knitted wool slippers but are actually buying slippers made from machine-knit wool from a factory in Arkansas.

Pros of Using Production Partners

There are endless benefits to using production partners. They can make your life easier, help you expand your product offering, and help you stay relevant to customers without requiring you to spread yourself thin learning new techniques or buying new equipment. Just make sure you stay honest about where you source your stuff and who helps you create it.

Cons of Using Production Partners

There's not a lot of cons to using production partners, as long as you're honest. However, you'll always have the folks that want to buy directly from the person who sheared the wool, wove the wool on the loom, and stitched it into their product, and these customers probably won't buy from you. But that's okay.

Stuff We Learned the Hard Way

The most important lessons I've learned the hard way over the years when it comes to supply chain and quality are as follows:

Failing to realize that drop shipping was a thing and how it could help me test out new grand ideas without breaking the bank to invest in new equipment.

Feeling confident that I was getting a steal of a deal on my supplies—without bothering to do my homework on whether or not that hypothesis was true. For a while, I was purchasing my supplies at WAY higher prices than I should have been. I didn't ask about discounts (I didn't know you could!), and I didn't shop around much because it was a pain in the butt. When I finally did, I kicked myself.

I've always tried to sell the BEST quality stuff I possibly could, but I've learned over the years that sometimes my customers have different ideas about what is most important to them. For instance, I was selling a more expensive sweater in my shop for a while that required special care. Most people didn't listen and washed it the wrong way (and damaged it). They were happier with a slightly lower quality item that was easier to care for. Evaluate quality through your customer's eyes, not yours.

CHAPTER 5

Selling through Your Own Site–Pattern by Etsy

For the vast majority of Etsy sellers, their shops are side hustles that bring in a little "fun money" and nothing more. For these sellers, Etsy's main platform is enough. But this is not you. I know because you're reading a book on how to turn your Etsy shop from hobby to business. This chapter talks about expanding beyond the standard Etsy shop—to Etsy's Pattern. Pattern is a great next step into the wide world of ecommerce that allows you to consolidate all your orders within the Etsy dashboard but gives you more freedom in what you sell and how you display your products to the world.

In the final chapter of this book, we'll talk about other ecommerce platforms totally beyond Etsy. But for now, let's focus on Pattern. Because it's such a natural, easy first step as a foray into ecommerce beyond Etsy.

Here are the pros and cons of adding a Pattern site. It won't be for everyone, but it's a great way to test how well your shop might succeed off Etsy's platform without the overhead of running two shops on two separate platforms.

Each of Pattern's features comes with pros and cons, e.g., having your own domain is awesome but brings extra costs. And customization is great, but there are definitely limits. Let's explore the different pros and cons to adding a Pattern site in depth.

Pro: Your Own Domain

This is the biggest benefit to adding a Pattern site—you can now sell from your own domain, a custom URL with your brand name, as well as through Etsy's platform. And on your end, sales from both sites flow through Etsy. That means you can still print labels, manage convos, and do everything, with a Pattern order exactly as you would with a straight-up Etsy order.

Selling through your own domain (ours is www.fourthwaveapparel.com) lends credibility to your shop because customers see that you're professional and established enough to have a legit web presence outside of Etsy. It also helps Google and other major search engines recognize your shop as an online store in its own right, separate from Etsy. Another perk of having your brand name in your URL is that your brand name becomes associated with the product you sell. Kleenex = tissue. Fourth Wave Apparel = awesome screen printed feminist shirts! That's what we're working toward, anyway.

Having your own domain can also give you an edge for running ads on Facebook or Instagram since you can place a "pixel" (a tracker essentially) on your Pattern site to gauge how well your ads are performing. You may find that different audiences respond more favorably to a traditional website than Etsy as well, depending on your product!

Con: Extra Costs

Owning your own URL does have a few downsides, though. For one, you've got to purchase the domain separately through a *domain name registrar* for a yearly fee. Etsy doesn't help with this step, nor offer much guidance on how to do it properly. And there are like a million companies out there that want to sell you a domain, so it can seem overwhelming. Most of these companies offer *web hosting services* (which you do NOT need to sell with Pattern), so you really have to go into the process knowing exactly what you're after: namely, JUST a domain purchase through a **domain registrar**.

I'll say it again because this is key: To create a Pattern site, you *only need a domain*. Etsy provides all the hosting services through its platform.

So, unless your business plan involves hiring a developer to build you a completely unique site later on, buy your domain from a *registrar* rather than a *hosting service*. Domain.com and GoDaddy.com are probably the most popular registrars out there and are great options. We use NameCheap.com, which is perfect for us. If you DO decide to use a hosting company (BlueHost, InMotion, GreenGeeks...), go into the exchange with the mindset you use when renting a car. They'll try to upsell you at every turn. Don't let them.

The only real reasons to go with a web hosting company rather than just a registrar is if you think you might want to start a specialized WordPress site (one with extra integration options that uses WordPress software but not WordPress hosting) alongside your shop. Or if you want to eventually hire a web designer to make you a website from scratch (or build a site yourself). Both of these options require third-party web hosting. If, however, you think you may want to leave Etsy and Pattern for Shopify or Squarespace, you still won't need web hosting because both companies provide it through their platforms. Even if you want to build your own site using a website builder (like Gater, Weebly, or Wix just to name a few), you don't need web hosting because all of the most popular site builders offer hosting with the monthly fee.

Pro: Pattern is Super Easy to Set Up and Use

Once you have your domain name, setting up Pattern is delightfully simple. I've worked on sites on a number of different platforms from Wordpress and Wix to Shopify and Squarespace, and Pattern is hands down the easiest I've ever set up and used. This is largely because Etsy fills in your Pattern site automatically with listings from your Etsy store. You simply choose a template and *BAM!* your Pattern site is up and looking pretty darn good

Con: Minimal Customization Options

The downside to simplicity, as one would expect, is that you don't have much power to personalize your Pattern site. The actual HTML and CSS are totally untouchable with a Pattern site. You've got the option to choose from ten themes, and once you pick one, you're mostly stuck with the layout and look of the theme unless you pick a different one. Within a theme, you can change the font, text color, and the color of certain sections of the page, like the header, and you can toggle the search feature and visibility of your reviews on or off. That's pretty much the limit in personalizing the look of your page.

Pro: Your Branding, Not Etsy's

On your Pattern homepage and all of your listing pages, Etsy's branding is completely absent. The only evidence that your site has anything to do with Etsy is a bit of text at the bottom of the page that says "Powered by Etsy." (You'll see the same notice on sites powered by SquareSpace or Shopify). Having your brand front and center lends a lot of legitimacy to your shop as an online store in its own right rather than just one of thousands of Etsy stores.

Con: Bumpy Checkout Process for Customers

The checkout process in your Pattern site isn't exactly seamless, and here's where Etsy's branding DOES show through: Once a customer clicks "checkout," they're forced to *leave your domain* (boo!) and checkout through a payment processing site with Etsy's URL and Etsy's branding. Customers even have to register as an Etsy guest or login to their Etsy account to complete the purchase.

Pro: More Freedom to Sell Items that Don't Fit Etsy's Rules and Regulations

Once you get your Pattern site up, you have the option to choose where each listing is displayed—Etsy only, Pattern only, or both channels. This is especially helpful because Etsy allows sellers to sell items on Pattern that are not allowed in Etsy stores, like resold items and services like photo restoration, tailoring, and consulting. You still can't sell anything from the "prohibited" list, of course, but Pattern definitely gives sellers more freedom.

Pros: Integration with Marketing, Social, and Analytics Platforms

For nearly the first year of its existence, Pattern offered options to integrate with third-party services (like MailChimp), but many of them either didn't work or were listed as "Coming Soon!" Seriously irritating for those of us early adopters. By 2020, however, sellers can connect their sites to Mailchimp, a free (with paid tiers) email marketing platform, and add Google Conversion Tracking, a Facebook pixel, and Pinterest verification.

I'll give you a brief overview of what each of these options is good for to help you decide if they'd be helpful for you.

* Mailchimp integration: Integrating your Pattern site with Mailchimp allows you to create **pop-ups** within your site asking customers to sign up for your mailing list and gives you access to Mailchimp's **targeted email tools**. Basically, these tools allow you to set automated emails to go out to customers who abandon their carts and target emails about specific products to customers who have bought similar items before, among other things. For Pattern listings, Etsy sends out "thank you" emails about purchases with the same custom message included in emails sent out for Etsy shop sales, but none of the other targeted emails (abandoned cart discounts, etc.) are sent to Pattern customers.

Warning! If you already are doing email marketing successfully, there's no obligation to integrate your Pattern site with Mailchimp. In fact, it's probably more work than it's worth to try to integrate an already established Mailchimp account with a new Pattern site. Because Mailchimp limits free accounts to one "audience," and Pattern wants to create a new one during the integration process, you either have to upgrade or delete your Mailchimp audience (while saving the emails in an Excel file or something) and essentially start over, which means losing all your analytics reports from previous campaigns.

- **Google Conversion Tracking:** This is a free service offered by Google to specifically track conversions, a term that means the number of people that buy your stuff out of all the people that see it. Once you know how to use the data, conversion tracking can help you make smart decisions about which listings to promote when and how best to market your products.

- **Facebook Pixels:** Like Google Conversion Tracking, the Facebook Pixel analyzes what's happening with purchases on your site. It tracks information about customers like demographic information, what they look at and how long, and what they end up purchasing with the end goal of focusing your Facebook ads toward the right group of people. If you have an active Facebook account and run ads, and especially if you're a verified business on Facebook, the pixel can do incredible things for your sales by showing your ads only to people who are most likely to purchase what you're advertising.

- **Pinterest Verification:** Connecting your Pinterest account to your website helps you become a Verified Pinterest Merchant, which gives you special privileges in the Pinterest community. For one, your account will have a special badge that lets viewers know you've been vetted and are a legitimate company. And Pinterest also gives advertising perks to its Verified Merchants like better and more frequent ad placement targeted to viewers who Pinterest believes would be interested in buying your products.

Con: Limited Ability to Integrate (Beyond Integrations Above)

Beyond the integrations mentioned above, Etsy doesn't allow Pattern sellers to connect their sites to Google search console or use any external analytics or marketing packages. You can't install add-ons or plug-ins like you can in Wordpress. There's no option to integrate with an Instagram account or other social channels beyond FaceBook and Pinterest. In other words, you're stuck with the limited selection Etsy offers in Pattern's "Marketing" shop section.

Pro: Etsy Customer Service (for Sellers)

Etsy has improved its customer service for sellers a lot over the life of the company. They now have a chat feature (YES!!) that sellers can use to get help and answers to problems quickly, and the customer service reps are polite, helpful, and knowledgeable. And Etsy has always used the Etsy forums very effectively for troubleshooting and for letting customers know when they're having a problem on the platform that affects sellers. What I'm saying is when you run into a problem setting up and running your Pattern site, there's fast and reliable help to be found.

Con: Slow Technical Support

While Etsy's communication is top-notch, unfortunately, their technical support, especially when it comes to Pattern, is still lacking. I think that Etsy may have stretched itself a little too thin when they decided to add Pattern and compete in the ecommerce platform market. Technical issues that come up don't get fixed very quickly, and there are some display problems in certain Pattern templates that the engineering team doesn't seem inclined to ever get around to fixing.

Since Pattern was offered to sellers as an option in 2016, sellers have found that their "Add to Cart" button is routinely broken (our customers were recently unable to purchase anything from our Pattern site for more than ten days—eek!). Hopefully, as Pattern grows (if it grows), Etsy's engineers will prioritize it more, but for now, slow fixes and some half-baked web coding are a few things to be aware of if you go down the Pattern route.

Pro: Minimal Costs

Etsy's Pattern site is free for the first month and costs $15 a month after that, which is less expensive than other options on the market (Squarespace, Shopify), and you only have to pay the $0.20 listing fee once for items listed on both Etsy and Pattern. Etsy has also recently eliminated transaction fees on items sold through Pattern as an extra incentive to sellers.

Con: You Still Have to Pay Shipping and Payment Processing Fees

Etsy still charges shipping fees and payment processing fees for items that sell on Pattern, so make sure to factor in these costs in your monthly budget for Pattern.

Things We Learned the Hard Way

When I decided to add a Pattern site, I'll admit I believed the process would be as simple as checking the button listing all my products on both my Etsy shop and my Pattern site. But it turns out that a shop optimized for Etsy search is very different from a site optimized for Google search. (And you want to focus on Google SEO rather than Etsy SEO on your Pattern site.) Below, I'll list some differences along with suggested solutions.

Titles: Etsy search rewards listings with longer titles made up of strings of relevant keywords. Google's search algorithm actively punished this behavior (called keyword stuffing).

Solution: Within each listing, check the box (found just under the description) "Edit my title and description for my Pattern site." This will allow you to edit your title and description specifically for listings displayed on your Pattern site. It'll take some time, but it's worth it. Not only will it allow your listings to rank higher in Google search, but shorter titles also look better on the Pattern site.

Descriptions: Descriptions on Etsy are largely for customers since Etsy's search algorithm doesn't consider them when deciding where to rank a listing for a given search. But Google's search algorithm does consider the first 150 words of the listing description.

Solution: Modify the first 150 words of your Pattern description based on keywords that customers might search for in a Google search (make sure to still use natural language though—no keyword stuffing!). This is a good place to include "handmade" and related keywords that are obvious to customers on Etsy's platform but might make your listing stand out in a Google search. There are some decent free "keyword volume tools" and "google rank checker tools" you can use to find the best keywords for getting your Pattern listing to rank in Google search. Paid tools like those from Moz.com are more accurate but probably not worth the price.

Troubleshooting: As I said above, troubleshooting even significant problems with your Pattern site can be difficult and time-consuming. The technical support team doesn't seem able to keep up with support requests, making Pattern somewhat unreliable as an ecommerce platform.

Solution: An Etsy shop alone can take you a long way. It's not necessary to ever have a Pattern site also. But if you do decide to use Pattern, I'd suggest it not become the main source for your sales. If you want to expand into having your own online store and perhaps leave Etsy behind, you will want to consider a platform whose whole existence is centered around making sure your ecommerce site works all the time. Some of the most popular of these platforms are discussed in the next chapter. Onward!

67

CHAPTER 6

Etsy vs. Other Ecommerce Platforms

If you're reading this book, you're likely already an Etsy seller or are strongly considering opening an Etsy shop. So I'm not here to pitch Etsy to you (any more than I already have, anyway). We've made it pretty clear that we're fans of Etsy as an ecommerce platform and have had a lot of success there. But I know that many Etsy sellers have questions about what else is out there in the world of ecommerce. So, as we wrap up, I want to give you a quick overview of the type of business that does well on Etsy (and on Etsy plus Pattern) so you can either feel confident that Etsy is the right place for you, or you can make the leap elsewhere.

So, let's jump into an overview of several of the other big-hitter ecommerce platforms and what they have to offer, specifically, SquareSpace, Shopify, and Amazon. After that, I'll also recommend some third-party integrations that can make your life SO much easier if you decide to sell across multiple platforms.

Etsy

Long story short, Etsy is an ideal selling platform for anyone who makes their products by hand. It has a reputation as an online market for boutique-style, mom-and-pop shops selling handmade items. Customers shop on Etsy knowing prices will be a bit higher and shipping times a bit longer but that they'll be able to find totally unique, high-quality handmade goods.

Because of Etsy's policies aimed at supporting small sellers, you can still make money even if you sell very few items and even if your shop is more of a hobby than a job. Etsy's seller platform is also very easy to use even if you're not tech-savvy, and Etsy will take care of advertising for you also.

Takeaway: Etsy is ideal for handmade-centric, smaller shops where the seller often strives to make personal connections to customers through unique, creative products.

Etsy Plus Pattern:

Selling on Etsy alone is great, but it can be discouraging when customers don't remember your Shop Name because you're "just another Etsy shop." Adding a Pattern site can add legitimacy and is a great tool for branding. Not only is your company name all over your homepage, but it's also the website address that customers type into Google search or the URL bar to find you, meaning they can get to your shop directly. And because your Pattern shop is basically your already-created Etsy shop displayed differently, setting up your Pattern site is incredibly simple.

Squarespace

Squarespace is another excellent ecommerce platform aimed at helping small businesses market and sell online. It may be a good option for a seller who feels she's outgrown Etsy and wants more freedom, someone who wants to sell services in addition to (or instead of) products (Etsy doesn't allow the sale of most services on its platform), or a seller who prefers to sell in person—for example at boutiques, craft fairs, or trade shows.

One of the main strengths of Squarespace's platform is how incredibly image-focused it is. Squarespace websites tend to be eye-catching and serve very well as online catalogues of the beautiful products you're offering at your next in-person event and that customers can browse before your next trade show. Squarespace templates also allow sellers to advertise in-person events in ways that are sure to catch customer's eye.

Squarespace also has excellent integration with social media platforms, so if you're already advertising on FaceBook and Instagram, and your photography is one of your shop's best assets, it may be a great fit for you.

Like I said above, Squarespace's template options and integrations make it a great option for those selling services rather than products, largely because the platform was created with service-focused businesses in mind. The majority of templates are aimed at meeting the needs of lawyers, restaurants, hair stylists, etc. So, if you want to sell, say consulting services alongside your products, Squarespace is an excellent option for that.

Squarespace is the most expensive ecommerce platform mentioned in this overview ($30/mo for the platform plus $9/mo for shipping integration, which is really necessary if you're selling products), so you definitely don't want to try it if your business is just a small side hustle. Because it uses a third party for sales (Stripe) and shipping (ShipStation), actually fulfilling orders for a SquareSpace shop is more cumbersome than it is in other ecommerce platforms.

It also takes substantially more time to set up and maintain. There are a variety of template options, and building the site is fairly user-friendly for the non-technical person, but it does allow sellers to make changes in the website code—specifically the structure (HTML) and the aesthetics (CSS), so it may be necessary to learn some basic coding at some point.

Shopify

Another platform to consider if you want to expand beyond what Etsy offers someday is Shopify. Shopify is by far the most popular ecommerce platform on the internet. It's clean, contemporary templates are ideal for selling products, which was why Shopify was created. Shopify's ecommerce tools are definitely its best feature. Customers can pay online through Stripe and PayPal and in-person through Shopify's Pay-on-site iPhone feature. And Shopify comes with shipping tools that make calculating shipping costs and printing labels easy and even give sellers shipping discounts up to 60%.

A basic Shopify account costs $30/month and includes everything you need to sell products online, including easy social media integration for marketing purposes. As with Squarespace, selling on Shopify isn't a step to take if your business is a side hustle. And like Squarespace, sellers can modify the website code, so some technical skills may end up being necessary.

Shopify's excellent customer service is one feature that makes it stand out among other ecommerce platforms. The platform is known for its responsiveness and customer support. So, if you're worried about taking the jump to a new ecommerce platform and would love some extra help, Shopify is a great option.

Amazon

This chapter wouldn't be complete without mentioning Amazon. Because of its size and reach, Amazon is a great platform for ecommerce. A lot of sellers do very well selling on Amazon.

That being said, it's hard for me to recommend Amazon to Etsy sellers. Amazon's business model and reputation are just so different from Etsy's, and the company is known for some borderline unethical practices toward its sellers, stuff like forcing sellers to have really low margins in order to even rank in search, unexpectedly lowering the percentage sellers keep from each sale, and even worse, stealing a product idea and selling it under "Basics by Amazon" for less than the original. Also, Amazon is so well known that there are actually apps out there that track the best prices and ratings on its products. Competition is fierce.

Customers come to Amazon expecting to find fast shipping, lower prices, and brands they can't find in their local stores. They're not necessarily coming to Amazon for handmade items, and they may not be willing to pay extra for these types of products.

Sellers who often do well on Amazon are drop-shippers who sell tens of thousands of their product at lower profit margins and people who sell very niche items customers can't find anywhere else (specialty tools or hardware, for example). It's worth noting that for broad-market items (for example, clothes or household items), Amazon prioritizes its own products over third-party listings.

Amazon also rewards sellers with very short shipping times. Amazon offers 2-3 day shipping on most of its products, and third-party sellers are expected to offer similar shipping times. This means keeping a stock of product on hand all the time or using Amazon's "Fulfilled by Amazon" tool, which allows sellers to send products to Amazon to store and ship out when orders come through.

Like Etsy, an Amazon account is free to set up. Amazon just charges sellers transaction fees when items sell, but no listing fees. If you take advantage of all the "extras" Amazon offers, however, (like warehouse space or advertising), the costs can wrack up quickly. If you want to give selling through Amazon a try, make sure you read over their "Sellers University" information *very* carefully.

Why Not Just Use ALL THE PLATFORMS?

Some sellers do sell on multiple platforms! But, as you can imagine, this can get expensive fast. Not to mention, a logistical game of Tetris in how you spend your time and resources. The companies that can do this and still make a profit usually have a different business model than your average Etsy seller. The biggest difference is scale. Some sellers spend a lot of money selling on many different platforms and advertising like crazy, and it pays off because they sell tens of thousands of products. Even if their product margins are lower (as in the case for drop-shippers), they still make plenty of money to cover the platform and advertising fees. Think about it this way: these sellers are moving so much product that the fixed Etsy fees and $30-$40 a month for Shopify and Squarespace are easily covered with plenty to spare.

Those of us who sell on Etsy, on the other hand, often make the stuff we sell ourselves, usually by hand, which means selling 10,000 [insert your product here] in a month is out of the question without some significant restructuring and hiring (which can threaten to change the vibe of your shop). The average Etsy seller needs to sell far fewer products but with higher margins, and we can't afford to waste our profits selling on multiple platforms or advertising across the internet.

Does that mean Etsy sellers who start selling a lot of product regularly need to jump ship or add a second platform? Not necessarily. But it's definitely something to seriously consider. As this chapter has discussed, different platforms cater to different business types and different "levels" of scale, and Etsy simply was not created and is not set up to handle businesses that sell very large volumes of product regularly.

There is, of course, nothing wrong with either end of the business model spectrum. Whether you sell a few items for more or lots of items for less or are somewhere in-between, it's a good idea to recognize the model that fits your business because it'll impact which platform(s) you pick and how you go about advertising and even interacting with customers.

Easing Expansion with Third-Party Integrations

Let's say you DO decide to expand your web presence. That's awesome! Selling across multiple platforms is an incredible way to get your products out into the world and to brand your shop as a serious and growing business. It also means more sales and more income (woot!). But taking the leap onto even one additional platform besides Etsy can be so daunting. Now, you have to manage sales and fulfillment, listing uploads, customer service, etc. from two different platforms, often *doubling* the amount of time you spend on the often less pleasant aspects of running a business. And that's not even taking into account the time you need to spend learning how a new platform works.

The good news is that you're not the first person to have this problem. It's been solved. And the solution is *integrations*. Integrations are tools that will automate different parts of your business for you or help two separate apps or tools work together more seamlessly. Think of some shop-related things that you'd rather not spend your precious time doing, say, posting to Instagram daily. There's an integration for that. Purchasing shipping labels? There's one for that too.

I couldn't list all available integrations here even if I wanted to. The really important thing is for you to understand the benefit of integrations, so that when you run into a process that's taking you far too much time, you can check the web for automation tools to solve your problem. That being said, here's a list of a few (out of hundreds of) super useful third-party tools you can use to automate your business processes across multiple platforms. Many of these tools integrate specifically with Etsy, while others integrate with useful platforms like social media.

- **ShipStation:** This service integrates well with all of the major ecommerce platforms including Etsy (and Pattern). It pulls shipping information for your customers from all of your sites and allows you to purchase shipping labels in big batches rather than getting labels for each of your platforms separately. ShipStation is most useful if you have an Etsy shop AND use another ecommerce platform like Shopify.

- **Later:** Through Later, you can schedule social media posts across multiple platforms. You just need to spend an hour or so once a week choosing or creating content, and Later will post for you at your pre-scheduled times, meaning your audience will see you as highly engaged, but you don't have to be glued to your social accounts all day everyday.

- **MailChimp:** We talked a lot about this email marketing tool in Book 2, but it's worth mentioning here as well. You can create a MailChimp landing page that offers willing subscribers a coupon code for your Etsy store. Then, you can send marketing emails out to these customers and increase your Etsy shop traffic (and sales).

- **Facebook Pixels:** If you place a Pixel onto your ecommerce site, FaceBook will track the behavior of your customers so you can target ads directly to them on your social media accounts. Pixels give you a lot more information about who's actually buying your stuff and lead to much higher conversion rates for your ads.

- **Survey Monkey:** Customers love to give you their opinions, and Survey Monkey is a great tool for creating questionnaires that you can send out to see what your customers like and don't like about your shop. You can even integrate Survey Monkey with your MailChimp account, so the surveys look like official emails from your business account.

- **Zapier:** This is the mother of all integration tools. Zapier is a service that integrates integrations—basically, it connects tools and sites that don't already work together. Let's say you want the answers to your survey questions to flow seamlessly into a Google Sheets spreadsheet so you can sort the data. But Survey Monkey and Google Sheets don't work like that. Zapier will integrate them for you. The service now has 300+ options for "Zaps" and is adding more every day.

Takeaway: With ecommerce integrations, you don't have to struggle through the onerous tasks of running a business. There are tools to help you out. Stop burning the midnight oil and put more of your processes on auto-pilot.

GET OUT THERE AND ETSY!

slaps you on the butt

Okay team. Before we break this huddle and you go build your Etsy empire, I just want to say this:

You absolutely CAN do this. Take it a step at a time, listen to solid advice, listen to your own data, iterate small, don't be afraid to grow (smartly), and never EVER let anyone tell you that you have a "little hobby." Etsy is an incredible platform filled with potential and it's only going to grow. Because of shops like yours and mine.

I spent way too long undervaluing my ability to run my own business. I saw myself as a mom from Idaho with a "fun side hobby" for far too much time. And I know from talking to many Etsy shop owners and clients over the years that others often feel the same way.

But people who craft, and people who create art have what it takes. I know this to be true, and I love what I do in helping other artists and crafters and makers see their own potential to follow their passion and do what they love for a living.

So, get out there and do the thing!

One last thing: Like we mentioned at the beginning of the book, if you'd like to enroll in the University of Etsy (by yours truly, CraftRanker!) as a companion to this book, you'll find more than 90 in-depth instructional videos and worksheets that enhance and reinforce book learning and help you apply what you've learned here about starting a successful Etsy shop. These standalone video courses are a $247 value at full price, but we're offering them as a learning companion to our readers at just 19.99. You'll find that offer here:

craftranker.com

Made in the USA
Monee, IL
15 November 2024

70223321R00049